Picture credits:
l: Left, r: Right, t: Top, b: Bottom, c: Centre

Front Cover Images: Background: Tamir Niv/ Shutterstock, ml: Olga Skalkina/ Shutterstock,
mr: Tomasovic_net/ Shutterstock, mc: Oliver Johannes Uhrig/ Shutterstock,
bl: Mikael Damkier/ Shutterstock, br: Larry St. Pierre/ Shutterstock
Back Cover Images: Background: ArtmannWitte/ Shutterstock, t: ©Airbus 2007-Fixion-Avianca,
ml: Stuart Taylor/ Shutterstock, b: Gusev Mikhail Evgenievich/ Shutterstock,
Border Images: Terry Chan/ Shutterstock, Larry St. Pierre/ Shutterstock, Mikael Damkier/ Shutterstock,
J. Helgason/ Shutterstock., Dmitry Bomshtein/ Shutterstock.

Inside: 12t: Tamir Niv/ Shutterstock, 14tl: Baloncici/ Shutterstock, Whaldener Endo/ Shutterstock,
14mr: Matt Ragen/ Shutterstock, 14br: Alex Staroseltsev/ Shutterstock,
15b: James M Phelps, Jr/ Shutterstock, 16-17m Tim Jenner/ Shutterstock, 18t: © Airbus S.A.S. 2007,
18b: Bugatti Automobiles S.A.S, 19t: © 2007 Shelby Supercars, LLC., 20ml: NASA,
19b: "WikipediaCommons Zache" 21t: NASA,
21mr: Motorola Archives, 21bl: © Apple Inc., 22t: NASA, 22b: NASA, 23b : NASA,
24b: Library of Congress Washington, 26br: istockphoto, 27m: Stuart Taylor/ Shutterstock,
27b: stock.xchng, 29t: Thomas Nord/ Shutterstock, 30t: Rex Features,
31m: © Patrick Ward / Alamy, 31b: Florin Cirstoc/ Shutterstock, 34t: Associated Press, 34b: Rex Features,
35b: Associated Press, 36b: Supplied by Capital Pictures, 37bl: Associated Press,
38t : © Bettmann/Corbis, 38b : Richard Termine, 39t: "WikipediaCommons FlickreviewR",
39b: "WikipediaCommons Osamak", 40b: Tan Wei Ming/ Shutterstock,
41b: "WikipediaCommons Magicknight94",
42t: "WikipediaCommons GeeJo", 42b: Wildphotos.com, ,
43b: Gusev Mikhail Evgenievich/ Shutterstock.
Updated Design Skylar Everett

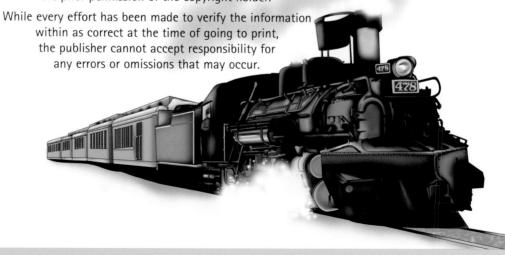

HUMAN ACHIEVEMENTS

CONTENTS

EARLIEST CIVILIZATIONS

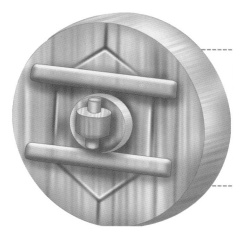

FIRST WHEEL AND PLOUGH

The Mesopotamians were the first to invent the wheel over 5,500 years ago! This was made of a block of wood and did not have any spokes. Metal nails or wooden pegs were used to attach it to a wooden cart. Around this time the Mesopotamians also invented the plough for farming. Made of wood, the plough was pulled by oxen and helped to revolutionize agricultural practices.

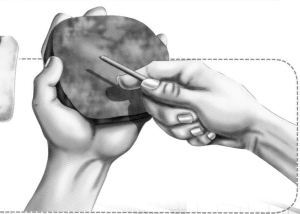

FIRST SCRIPT

The cuneiform script is the earliest form of written expression. The Sumerians of Mesopotamia created this around 3200 BC, mainly to keep an account of what they bought or sold. Cuneiform was actually a system of pictograms. Since paper had not yet been invented, the Mesopotamians drew the symbols on wet clay tablets with reeds.

FIRST URBAN SANITATION SYSTEM

The cities in the Indus Valley – a civilization that flourished between 2600-1700 BC – showed signs of the first urban sanitation system in the world. This sanitation and drainage system is evidence of the extraordinarily advanced engineering and technology of the area for the period. The main drain ran through the middle of the main street below the level of the pavement and was well covered with stone slabs and tile bricks. The individual drains of each house in the city were connected to the main drain. This in turn was connected to a larger sewerage, which helped to channel dirty water beyond the city boundary.

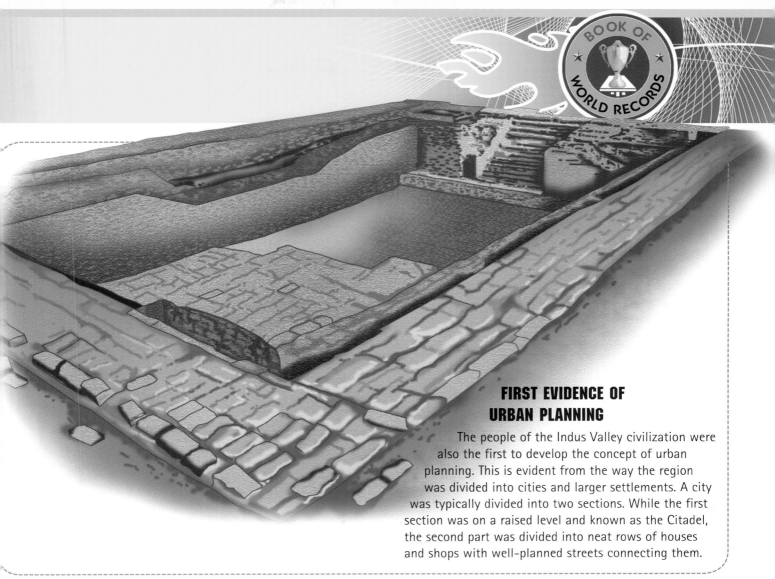

FIRST EVIDENCE OF URBAN PLANNING

The people of the Indus Valley civilization were also the first to develop the concept of urban planning. This is evident from the way the region was divided into cities and larger settlements. A city was typically divided into two sections. While the first section was on a raised level and known as the Citadel, the second part was divided into neat rows of houses and shops with well-planned streets connecting them.

INVENTORS OF BRONZE

The people living in the Mesopotamian region were skilled metal workers. The Sumerians first discovered bronze by mixing tin and copper in around 3000 BC. With this they made a variety of objects, such as daggers, tools, vessels and figurines.

Did you know?

The Mesopotamians were also the first to write stories! *The Epic of Gilgamesh* was written more than 4,000 years ago. Written on 12 clay tablets, this story narrates the exciting adventures of Gilgamesh and his friend Enkidu.

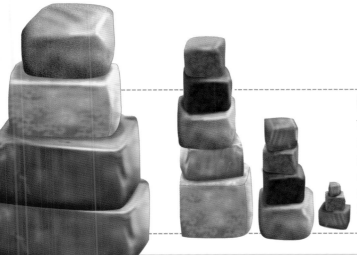

FIRST SYSTEM OF UNIFORM WEIGHTS

The people of the Indus Valley are credited with devising the first system of uniform weights and measures. Their measurements were very precise and they also followed a decimal system very closely. Brick sizes were in a ratio of 4:2:1 and weights were also uniform with each unit weighing 28 g (0.9 oz).

FIRST WRITING SYSTEM

The world's first known writing system, the Egyptian hieroglyph, could be written both vertically and horizontally. Interestingly, the term 'hieroglyph' was not invented by the Egyptians, but by the Greeks, many years later in the 1st century BC. According to the ancient Egyptians, writing was invented by the god Thoth. So they called the script *mdwt ntr*, meaning god's words. The script is a mixture of picture symbols and phonetic characters. This script was mostly found on the walls of temples and tombs.

FIRST WRITING MEDIUM

Using the pith of the papyrus plant, papyrus was the earliest form of material used for writing. It was first used as early as 4000 BC in ancient Egypt. Once the Egyptians had mastered the technique of converting papyrus into a writing medium, they were secretive about the method so as to hold the monopoly over its export. However, with the discovery of paper in China in AD 105, papyrus making came to an end. It was only as recently as 1965 that an Egyptian scientist, Dr Hassan Ragab, rediscovered the technique.

FIRST SAILBOATS

The earliest boats used in Egypt were rafts made of logs or reeds strapped together. It was to these boats that the ancient Egyptians first added sails. The first sails (around 3500 B.C.) were square and caught the wind's power to move boats on the Nile River upstream since that was the way the wind blew. The boats were then paddled back downstream into the wind.

ORIGINS OF POTTERY

The earliest records of pottery and the development of the potter's wheel can be traced back to ancient Egypt, around 2500 BC. Although the potter's wheel was invented during the period of the Old Kingdom (2686–2181 BC), it is believed that the Egyptians made pottery even before the construction of pyramids. This is evident from older hieroglyphics and pictures of pottery and small earthen vessels found in tombs dating back to the 4th–6th century BC.

OLDEST ANCIENT WONDER OF THE WORLD

The pyramids of Egypt are one of the earliest surviving wonders of the ancient world. Built in different shapes and sizes from the beginning of the Old Kingdom (2686–2181 BC) to the end of the Middle Kingdom (2055–1650 BC), these pyramids were the tombs of the pharaohs and their queens. About 80 pyramids exist in Egypt today. The largest and the most well-known among these is the Great Pyramid of Khufu. The famous Step Pyramid at Djoser, built by Pharaoh Djoser around 2630 BC, was the first pyramid ever built in Egypt.

Did you know?

Ancient Egyptians not only invented our modern 365 day calendar but the leap year system as well. Prior to that, ancient civilizations marked time using a lunar calendar system. The first leap year established by the Egyptians was in 238 B.C.

OLDEST AND LARGEST STONE SCULPTURE

The Sphinx at Giza is the oldest and the largest stone sculpture in the world. With a human head and a lion's body, the sphinx represents a form of the ancient Sun God. Carved out of a single block of limestone, the gigantic figure is 185 ft (57 m) long, 20 ft (6 m) wide and 65 ft (20 m) high, making it the largest statue in the world to be carved out of a single piece of stone.

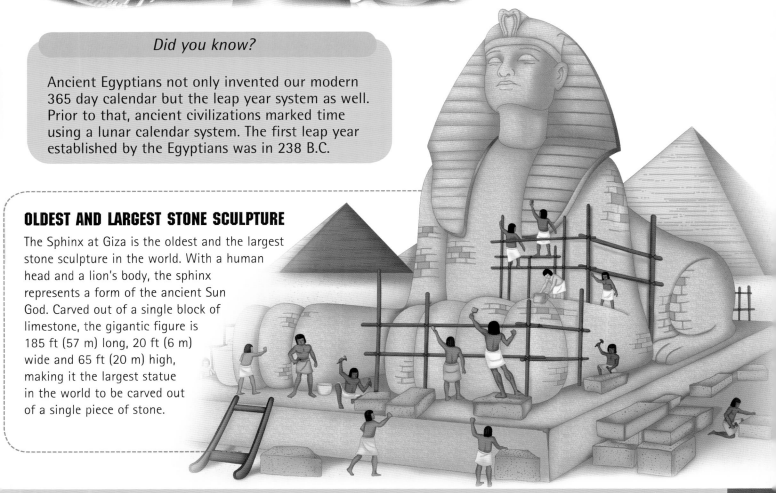

GREECE AND ROME

FIRST OLYMPICS

The Olympic games first started in Olympia, a town in ancient Greece, in 776 BC. The Olympics was one of four sporting events that marked important funeral ceremonies. The other three were the Isthimian, Nemean and Pythian games. The Olympics were originally held to honor the Greek god Zeus. Events such as chariot racing, wrestling, jumping, running and javelin throwing were held at the games. Only men were allowed to participate. The winners were given crowns made of leaves from a sacred olive tree, located near the Temple of Zeus in Olympia.

FIRST DEMOCRACY

The idea of democracy began in Athens, in ancient Greece. Athenian men could cast their votes and choose their leaders. However, this democracy was limited as not all citizens had the right to vote: only rich men born in Athens could participate. Women and slaves were not allowed to vote. Athens also had an interesting system, called ostracism, whereby an unpopular person was thrown out of the city if enough votes were collected against him!

WATER SCREW AND CLAW

Archimedes invented the first water screw — a device with a revolving screw-shaped blade inside a cylinder. This screw was originally designed to drain water from ships. But later it was adapted to help transfer water from low-lying water bodies to higher areas for irrigation. Archimedes was also the first to invent a crane. This crane, known as Archimedes's claw, had a hook attached to it that could be used to lift enemy ships out of the water!

FIRST LIGHTHOUSE

The ancient Greeks also built the first lighthouse of the world. This was the lighthouse of Alexandria located on the Island of Pharos. The brain behind it was Ptolemy Soter, a commander under Alexander the Great. The lighthouse was built in approximately 280 BC. It was a three-story structure (300 ft) 91.5 m high. The top level contained the beacon of fire that provided a warning light for the sailors. The lighthouse stood for 1,500 years, before collapsing during an earthquake in about 1220 AD!

THE FIRST USE OF STONE ARCHES IN BUILDING

The ancient Romans were great builders. In fact, they pioneered the use of arches. An arch is a curved structure that helps to spread load more evenly. Arches helped Roman architects a great deal. They could now build bridges across wide rivers, as well as aqueducts and spacious buildings.

FIRST HAT

The Greeks are said to have invented the first hat. This was the broad-brimmed *petasos*. This hat also had a chin strap. This allowed the wearer to hang the hat down the wearer's back when not in use. Ancient Greek men wore the hat when they travelled for long distances.

Did you know?

The catapult was first invented in ancient Greece in 399 BC, by Dionysius the Elder of Syracuse. It could hurl heavy objects or arrows over a large distance and was used as an effective weapon in war!

FIRST CONCRETE

The ancient Romans invented concrete in the 4th century BC. By chance, a Roman builder made a mushy paste with limestone and water. He then added sand, pebbles and stones to this mixture and stirred well. The mixture looked like a blob of grey material with lumps in it. It was now ready to be moulded into any shape. The Roman realized that when the mixture dried it became hard. Concrete thus helped the ancient Romans make durable roads and even aqueducts to supply water.

GREATEST WALL

The Great Wall of China is the only man-made structure on earth that is visible from space! The wall is over 4,000 miles (6,400 km) long. It took over a thousand years and more than a million people to build this incredible structure. The wall was built to prevent mass invasions and attacks from enemies.

WORLD'S LARGEST CONCENTRATION OF ROYAL TOMBS

The 13 tombs of the Ming Dynasty are said to be the world's largest concentration of royal tombs. Located 31 miles (50 km), northwest of the city of Beijing is an arc-shaped cluster of small hills where the 13 emperors of the Ming Dynasty were buried. The construction of the tombs started in 1409 and ended with the fall of the dynasty in 1604. The tombs were built on an area over 15 sq/miles over the 200 years. The area is commonly known as the Ming Tombs.

INVENTION OF PAPER

Although the Egyptians were the first to make papyrus, a paper-like material, the process of paper-making originated in ancient China and the Chinese are credited with developing paper as we know it today! Before inventing paper, the Chinese wrote by carving figures on pottery, stones, animal bones, wood and strips of silk. However, all these means of communication proved to be too expensive. The Chinese sought other cheaper materials until the first paper was made in Gansu province in China. However, it was Cai Lun who improvised on the initial findings and developed a more advanced form of paper using plant fibre. The first batch was presented to the Han Emperor in 105 AD and was called 'Marqui Cai's Paper'.

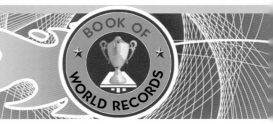

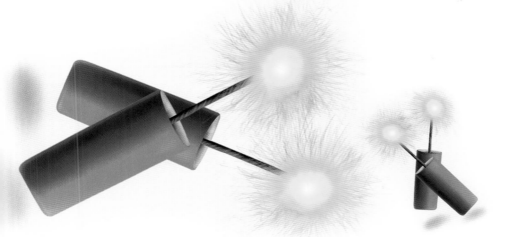

INVENTION OF THE COMPASS

A device called the SI-Nan, invented by the Chinese, was the forerunner of the modern day compass. It was first used during the Qin Dynasty (221-206 BC) by fortune tellers. The compass comprised of a magnetic lodestone with a bronze handle that always pointed to the south. This later gave way to magnetised needles during the eighth century AD, again in China. These were commonly used to help navigate ships. The first person known to have used the compass as a device for navigation was Zheng He from the Yunnan province in China.

FIRST TEA

Tea, now considered one of the most popular beverages in the world, started its journey in ancient China about 5,000 years ago. According to legend, an emperor called Shen Nung ordered that all water be boiled before drinking. It was during one such time that some leaves from a nearby bush fell into the boiling water, infusing it with a brown colour. The emperor found it to be an extremely refreshing drink. And so, tea came into being as a beverage as far back as 2737 BC!

FIRST CROPS

Mesoamericans were the first to cultivate many food crops, such as maize, chilli peppers, guavas, avocados and tomatoes. They also grew a large variety of potatoes and corn, unknown to other civilizations until then. Mesoamericans were also the first to cultivate the cacao tree. So popular was the tree that they even used the cacao beans as an early form of currency!

FIRST GUM AND RUBBER

Mesoamericans chewed the resin or gum of trees to clean their teeth and exercise their jawbones! Their favourite was chicle, the sap of the Sapodilla tree. Although this sticky sap was tasteless it is the substance from which modern day chewing gum was first made. Olmecs, a group of Mesoamericans, were the first to discover natural rubber.
In fact, they owe their nickname, 'rubber people', to this discovery. The Olmecs also discovered a way of treating rubber allowing them to make several items for daily use.

FIRST POPCORN AND CHOCOLATE DRINK

The Mesoamericans developed many delicious food that we still enjoy eating today. Corn was the staple food of the Mesoamericans. Since they needed a way of preserving it, they heated corn seeds and made the world's first popcorn! The Mesoamericans were also the first to make the first chocolate drink! They used cacao beans to make a frothy drink that was not sweet and warm, as we like it, but cold and bitter. It was flavoured with chilli and flower extracts! This mixture was drunk at weddings and during festivals.

GAMES PEOPLE PLAY

A popular game in the US and Canada, lacrosse originated in ancient America and was named by early French missionaries. This ancient game was an important part of native society, culture and religion. Unlike its modern version that is played by two teams consisting of 10 players each, in ancient America each team consisted of about 100 to 1,000 men on a huge field. The ancient Americans played this game not just as a form of entertainment but also to train young warriors. The game was often played to settle disputes between tribes.

LARGEST PYRAMID

The world's largest pyramid is not in Egypt, but in Mexico. Built between the 2nd and early 16th century BC, the Great Pyramid of Cholula is the largest in the world. This massive pyramid has a base of 1,476 sq/ft (450 sq/m) and rises to a height of 217 ft (66 m). It was built to honor the god Quetzalcoatl.

Did you know?

Ancient Americans invented one of the first calendars. The Mayan calendar consisted of 260 days and each day was given a name, much like our days of the week. Each day had a special symbol.

FIRST STEAM ENGINE

The first steam engine was developed by Thomas Newcomen in 1712 to help pump out excess water from coal mines. It was an extremely simple piston device and used large amounts of energy to draw out water. It was only later, in 1765, that a Scotsman named James Watt added a separate cooling chamber to the machine and devised the first sample of the modern steam engine that we know today. It was patented in 1769 and in 1776 the first engines were installed in commercial enterprises. By 1800 the steam engine had replaced water as the major source of power in Europe.

Did you know?

The Smethwick Engine is the oldest working steam engine. It was built in 1779, by James Watt and Mathew Boulton, to pump water in the Birmingham Canal at Smethwick, England.

FIRST STEAM LOCOMOTIVE

After James Watt improved the steam engine, many inventors tried to use it for a variety of purposes. Richard Trevithick successfully built a steam locomotive that could be used to haul a train. In 1804, his engine pulled a train loaded with 10 tons of iron and 70 passengers. Other inventors, such as Matthew Murray, William Hedley and George Stephenson improvised on Trevithick's engine and helped to build commercially successful trains.

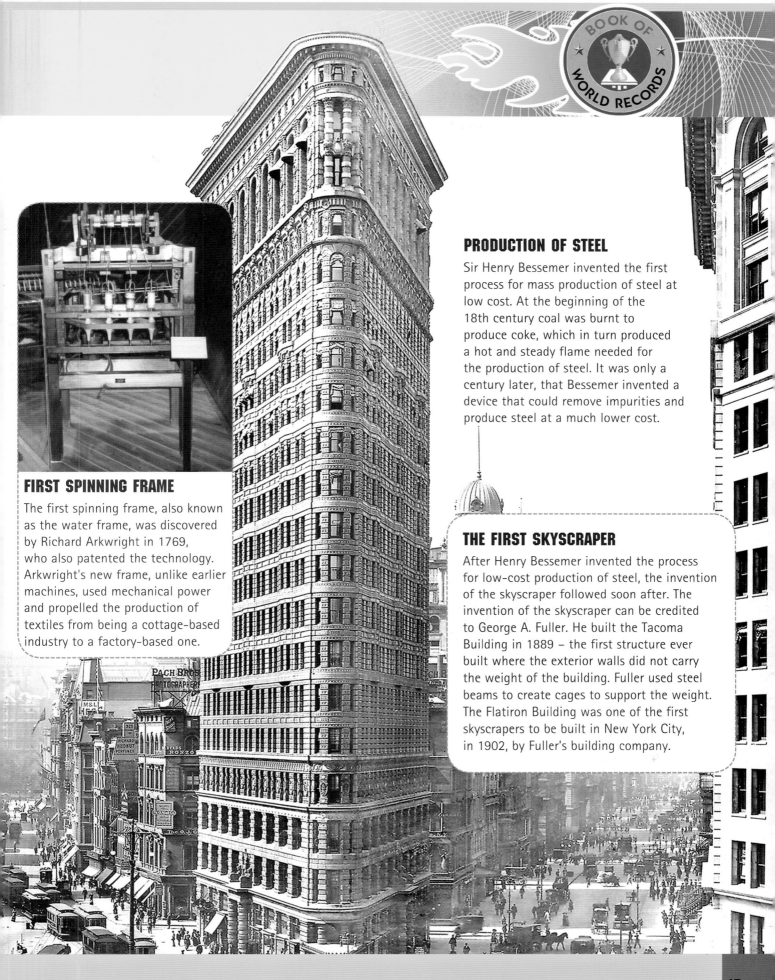

PRODUCTION OF STEEL

Sir Henry Bessemer invented the first process for mass production of steel at low cost. At the beginning of the 18th century coal was burnt to produce coke, which in turn produced a hot and steady flame needed for the production of steel. It was only a century later, that Bessemer invented a device that could remove impurities and produce steel at a much lower cost.

FIRST SPINNING FRAME

The first spinning frame, also known as the water frame, was discovered by Richard Arkwright in 1769, who also patented the technology. Arkwright's new frame, unlike earlier machines, used mechanical power and propelled the production of textiles from being a cottage-based industry to a factory-based one.

THE FIRST SKYSCRAPER

After Henry Bessemer invented the process for low-cost production of steel, the invention of the skyscraper followed soon after. The invention of the skyscraper can be credited to George A. Fuller. He built the Tacoma Building in 1889 – the first structure ever built where the exterior walls did not carry the weight of the building. Fuller used steel beams to create cages to support the weight. The Flatiron Building was one of the first skyscrapers to be built in New York City, in 1902, by Fuller's building company.

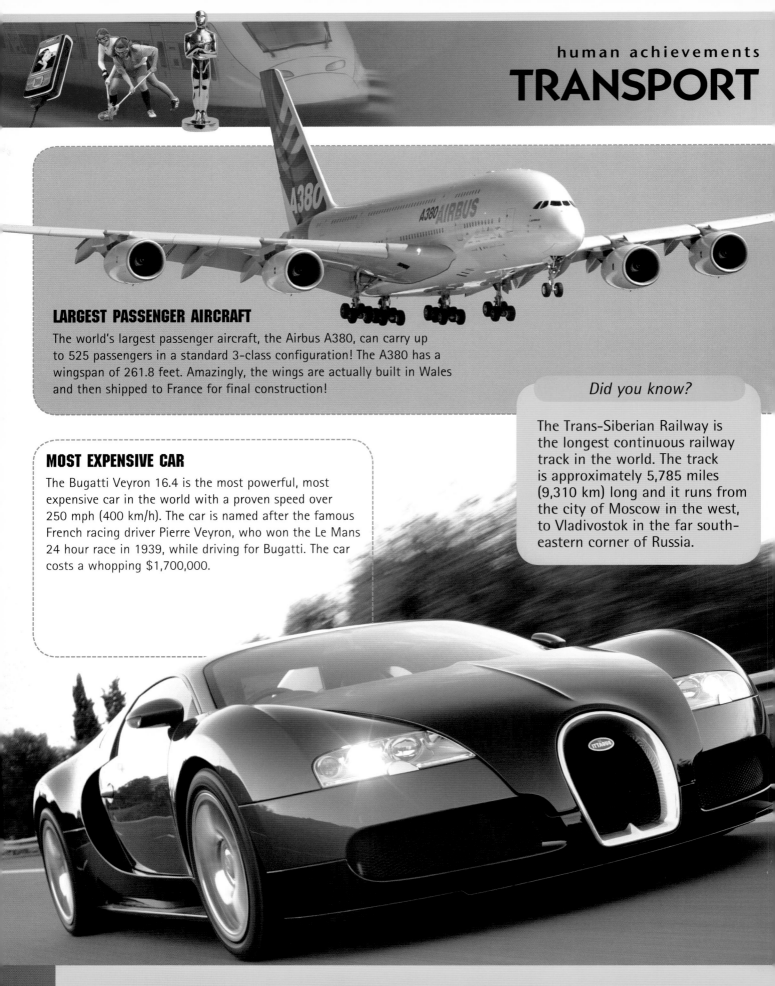

LARGEST PASSENGER AIRCRAFT

The world's largest passenger aircraft, the Airbus A380, can carry up to 525 passengers in a standard 3-class configuration! The A380 has a wingspan of 261.8 feet. Amazingly, the wings are actually built in Wales and then shipped to France for final construction!

Did you know?

The Trans-Siberian Railway is the longest continuous railway track in the world. The track is approximately 5,785 miles (9,310 km) long and it runs from the city of Moscow in the west, to Vladivostok in the far south-eastern corner of Russia.

MOST EXPENSIVE CAR

The Bugatti Veyron 16.4 is the most powerful, most expensive car in the world with a proven speed over 250 mph (400 km/h). The car is named after the famous French racing driver Pierre Veyron, who won the Le Mans 24 hour race in 1939, while driving for Bugatti. The car costs a whopping $1,700,000.

FASTEST CAR

The Ultimate Aero TT supercar, built by Shelby Super Cars, is the world's fastest production car. The car can achieve a top speed of 256 mph (412 km/h) and can accelerate from 0-60 mph in just 2.8 seconds! The Aero is a two-seater car with butterfly-style flip doors and a lightweight body made of carbon and titanium. The designers of the car spent over seven years working on the design, yet it's thought that only 25 will ever be made and sold!

LARGEST PASSENGER SHIP

The Monstrous Oasis of the Sea is the most gigantic passenger ship in the world - five times the size of the Titanic! The superliner is 1,181 feet long and can carry 5,400 passengers in 2,700 staterooms. The 215 foot tall behemoth has 2 six-story towers with a courtyard between them that is the size of a football field. This huge area is called Central Park because it is landscaped with 400 tons of plants and the soil to grow them.

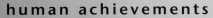

FIRST TELEPHONE

Alexander Graham Bell is generally credited with inventing the telephone. In the 1870s, Elisha Gray and Bell were working independently to make devices that would transmit speech as electrical signals. Both rushed to patent their devices, but Bell managed to patent his first! On 10 March, 1876, Bell's 'electrical speech machine', which we now call a telephone, was ready to be displayed. He made the first phone call to his assistant Thomas Watson, saying, 'Mr Watson, come here. I want to see you.'

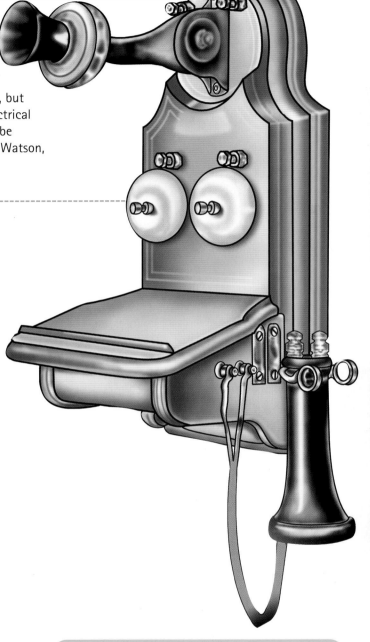

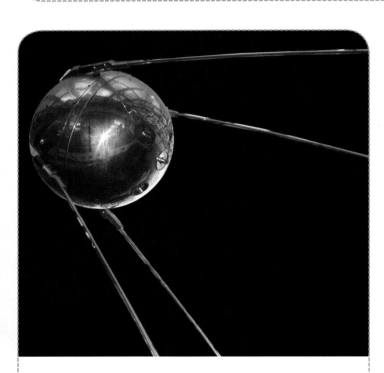

WORLD'S FIRST SATELLITE

Space knowledge and technology took a giant leap on 4 October, 1954. It was on this day that the Soviet Union successfully launched Sputnik I, the world's first artificial satellite. The small satellite, about the size of a beach ball, stunned the world when it was launched into the earth's orbit. The satellite travelled at 18,000 mph (29,000 km/h) and transmitted radio signals at 20.005 and 40.002 Megahertz for about 22 days, before the batteries ran out. The launch brought about far reaching developments in science and technology and triggered the so called 'space race' between the Soviet Union and the USA.

Did you know?

The world's first calculator was invented by Charles Babbage. Called the difference engine, this device used the decimal system and could be operated by cranking a handle.

WORLD'S FIRST COMPUTER

Charles Babbage is generally considered to be the father of computing. His analytical engine paved the way for future computers. The first purely electronic computer, capable of being programmed to solve a full range of computing problems, was the ENIAC. Short for Electronic Numerical Integrator and Computer, the ENIAC was constructed in 1943 in America and is the first functionally useful general purpose computer.

FIRST MOBILE PHONE

Bell's phone was big and bulky. Over the years many inventors sought to make it light and easy to carry. A revolution happened in the telecommunication industry with the invention of the mobile phone. The first mobile phones were not truly mobile as they could not be carried everywhere. The first truly portable, handheld mobile phone was introduced by Motorola on 3 April, 1973. It was designed by Motorola engineers Marty Cooper and John Mitchel. Although clunky by today's standards, it paved the way for future mobile phones.

COUNTRY WITH THE MOST MOBILE PHONE USERS

China has more than 500 million active mobile phone accounts. Luxembourg, however, tops the list of countries with the highest ratio of mobile phone users, with approximately 1.6 mobile phones per head. It's thought that there are more than 2.7 billion mobile phone users worldwide!

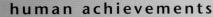
SPACE FIRSTS

FIRST MAN IN SPACE

The Russian cosmonaut, Yuri Gagarin, was the first man to travel into space. On April 12, 1961, he made a 108-minute orbital flight in his spacecraft, Vostok 1. Gagarin completed a full orbit of the earth and it was during this orbit that he was promoted from the rank of Senior Lieutenant to Major. After the successful completion of the flight, Gagarin became a worldwide celebrity and made many appearances in various parts of the world to promote the Soviet achievement.

FIRST MAN ON THE MOON

Neil Armstrong has the honor of being the first man to walk on the moon, on 20 July, 1969. Armstrong stepped onto the surface of the moon from the Apollo 11 spacecraft, uttering the historic words: 'This is one small step for man, one giant leap for mankind.' Neil Armstrong and his crew spent about two-and-a-half hours on the surface of the moon, collecting samples to take back to earth. They also left an American flag there as a reminder of the accomplishment. The moon walk was watched on television around the world with amazement.

FIRST SPACE STATION

The Soviet Union launched the first space station on April 19, 1971. Salyut 1 was launched to carry out research into the problems of living in space and other astronomical, biological and earth resources experiments.

Did you know?

Laika, a dog, was the first animal to be launched into space, in 1957. She survived the launch and remained in the earth's orbit for four days, but died in space when the air supply ran out.

FIRST WOMAN IN SPACE

Valentina Vladimirovna Tereshkova became the first woman in space, on board Vostok 6, launched in 1963. The spaceship made 48 orbits of the Earth and the flight lasted for 3 days. Tereshkova was honored with the title 'Hero of the Soviet Union' upon the completion of this historic mission.

FIRST SPACE SHUTTLE

The first space shuttle, Columbia, was launched in 1981. It completed 37 full orbits of the earth, flying 1,074,567 miles in 2 days, 6 hours, 20 minutes and 53 seconds, before returning to earth!

WARTIME INVENTIONS

LARGEST HELICOPTER

The world's largest helicopter was built by MIL, a Russian military company. The Mi-26 was designed along the same lines as the company's first helicopter, the Mi-6. The Mi-26 is more elegant, and currently also the most popular heavy-lift helicopter in the world. It was the first helicopter to have eight blades in its main rotor.

FIRST SUBMARINE

Corneilus van Drebbel, a Dutch inventor, built the first submarine in 1620. The first time a submarine was used for military warfare was in 1776 by David Bushnell; known as the *Turtle*, Bushnell's submarine was used during the American Revolution against British warships. Later, two rival inventors designed the first 'true submarine' in 1890. These submarines used petrol for cruising on the surface of water and electric motors while underwater.

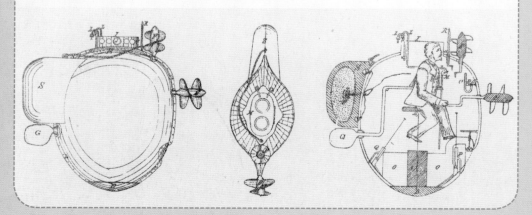

FIRST NUCLEAR ATTACK

The first and only nuclear attack that has ever taken place is the bombing of the two Japanese cities of Hiroshima and Nagasaki in August 1945. Two powerful atom bombs, code-named Little Boy and Fat Man, were dropped on the two cities by the American 12-man crew of the B-29 Superfortress bomber plane, Enola Gay. The event effectively ended World War II. The atomic bombings of Hiroshima and Nagasaki are widely considered the worst attacks in world history. The bombs killed hundreds of thousands and the long-term effects of the radiation fall-out are still being felt today.

Did you know?

World War II was the costliest and worst war in world history. The total number of fatalities is estimated to have been 50 million people, including both civilian and military deaths.

LARGEST AIRCRAFT CARRIER

The USS *Ronald Reagan* is the world's largest aircraft carrier. The ninth ship in the Nimitz-class aircraft supercarrier range is a nuclear-powered vessel, capable of accommodating 6,000 naval staff and more than 80 warplanes. The ship's two nuclear reactors are capable of propelling the ship for more than 20 years without the need to refuel!

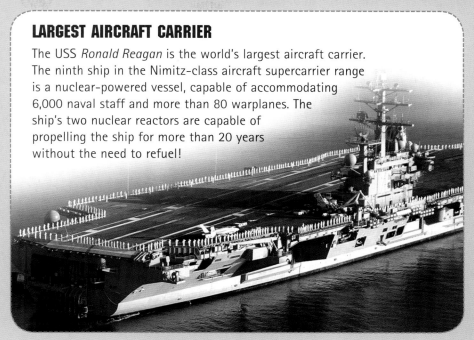

LARGEST BATTLESHIPS

Yamato and *Musashi*, the Japanese battleships of World War II, were the biggest battleships ever constructed. Built at Kure, Japan, both *Yamato* and *Musashi* were the main weapons of the Japanese Navy during World War II. On October 24, 1944, while *Musashi* was on its way to the Leyte landing beach, it was attacked by the US Navy. It took 20 torpedoes and 17 bombs to finally sink this monstrous ship. *Yamato* set sail for the last time in April 1945. The ship was a part of Operation Ten-Go and had been dispatched to attack the American fleet. It was hit by about 20 bombs and torpedoes, before the ship's ammunitions blew up — sinking it in the process.

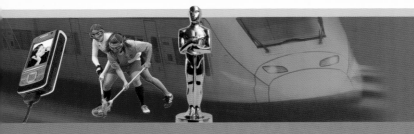

TALLEST HOTEL

The Burj al Arab is the world's tallest structure to be used as a hotel. The hotel is located in the United Arab Emirates and is constructed on a man-made island about 919 ft (280 m) away from the coast. In Arabic, its name means 'tower of the Arabs'. Shaped like a giant sail, the Burj al Arab has been built in such a way that its shadow does not fall on the beach nearby. The impressive 60-storey hotel consists of over 200 duplex suites and even has a helipad on its roof!

LARGEST STADIUM

The Mayday Stadium, also called Rungnado May First Stadium, in North Korea, is the largest sports stadium in the world. This stadium has a seating capacity of 150,000. It has eight floors and is over 197 ft (60 m) high. The Mayday Stadium has 16 arched roofs arranged in a ring that are designed like the petals of a flower.

TALLEST BUILDING
AND SO MUCH MORE!

The world's tallest building is the 2,717 foot (828m) tall Burj Kalifia in Dubai, United Arab Emirates. At it's opening on January 4, 2010 it gained the official titles of; Tallest Skyscraper in the World, Tallest Structure Ever Built, Tallest Freestanding Structure, World's Highest Elevator Installation, World's Fastest Elevator Speed, World's Highest Swimming Pool and World's Highest Outdoor Observation Deck to name but a few.

Did you know?

When it opened on May 1, 1931 the Empire State Building was the tallest building in the world standing at 1,250 feet tall. At the time, the building of the 57 story Empire State Building was considered an impossible task.

TALLEST TWIN TOWERS

The Petronas Towers are the world's tallest twin towers. They were also the world's tallest buildings, until the Taipei 101 overtook them by 184 ft (56 m). Each tower is 88 storeys high and has over 30,000 windows! A 190 ft- (58 m) long double-deck sky bridge connects the two towers at the 41st and 42nd floors.

LARGEST BUILDING IN THE WORLD

The Boeing Company's Factory in Everett, Washington is the largest building in the world by volume. At 1472 cubic feet it covers 98.3 acres. In this factory, Boeing builds 747's, 767's, 777's, and the new 787 Dream Liner Airplanes.

Human Achievements

BRIDGES AND TUNNELS

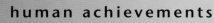

LONGEST RAIL TUNNEL

The Seikan Tunnel is the longest railway tunnel in the world. It is 33.49 miles (53.85 km) long, of which 14.5 miles (23.3 km) is under the sea. The Seikan Tunnel connects the two islands of Honshu and Hokkaido in Japan. Until the Seikan Tunnel was built, the only way to cross the Tsugaru Strait between the two islands was by ferry. In 1954, five ferries sank during a typhoon. More than 1,400 people died, causing public outrage and prompting the government to build the tunnel as a safer alternative.

LONGEST ROAD TUNNEL

The world's longest road tunnel cuts through the Alpine mountain range. The 15.3 mile (24.5 km) long Laerdal Tunnel in Norway provides a shorter route between the cities of Bergen and Oslo and is also a safer alternative to the narrow route up the mountains. One of the tunnel's unique features is the three mountain 'halls': these allow vehicles to turn back in case of fire at the other end. Alarm systems too have been installed to warn of danger.

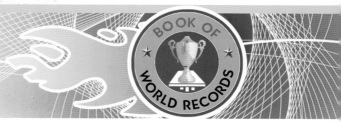

WIDEST BRIDGE

The Sydney Harbour Bridge is the widest bridge in the world. The road on the bridge is called the Bradfield Highway. The bridge consists of eight lanes for road traffic, two railway tracks and a bicycle lane. The Sydney Harbour Bridge is fondly known as the 'coathanger' in Australia.

LONGEST SUSPENSION BRIDGE

The Akashi Kaikyo Bridge is the world's longest suspension bridge. The central span of the bridge is 6,532 ft (1,991 m) long. The 928 ft (283 m) bridge towers of the Akashi Kaikyo are taller than any other in the world. The bridge has tuned mass dampers that sway in the opposite direction of the wind. This neutralizes the effect of winds as strong as 180 mph (290 km/h)! Originally the bridge was supposed to serve both rail and road traffic. However, by the time the construction began it was decided to restrict the bridge to road traffic only.

Did you know?

The Thames Tunnel in London, England was the world's first-ever underwater tunnel. The tunnel was built over a period of 18 years. The Thames Tunnel was originally built for carriages. It was converted into a railway tunnel in 1865 and became a part of the London Underground in 1913.

LONGEST STEEL ARCH BRIDGE

The Lupu Bridge in Shanghai, China, is currently the world's longest steel-arch bridge. The 1,805 ft (550 m) arch is about 105 ft (32 m) longer than the New River Gorge Bridge in West Virginia, US, which had held the title since 1977. The arch of the Lupu Bridge is made up of 27 segments. The 2.4 mile (3.9 km) long bridge stretches across the Huangpu River in Shanghai.

MOST EXPENSIVE PAINTING BY AN OLD MASTER

The Massacre of the Innocents by Peter Paul Rubens made history when it sold for an astonishing price of $76.73 million in May 1989. The work, painted in 1611, sold for more than double the price of the previous record-holding old master – Rembrandt's *Portrait of a Lady*, which fetched $28.7 million. Third in the list is *Portrait of Omai*, by Sir Joshua Reynolds. This painting sold for $14.6 million dollars in 2001. The art world defines work by old masters as paintings completed before 1800.

MOST EXPENSIVE PAINTING BY A LIVING ARTIST

Jasper Johns holds this record with the three paintings that top this list. His *False Start* fetched a whopping $80 million in 2006 — the highest ever for a contemporary painting! *False Start* was previously sold for $17 million in 1988.

Did you know?

Rembrandt's portrait of the famous Dutch engraver Jacob III de Gheyn has been stolen four times since 1966! It is jokingly known as the 'Takeaway Rembrandt'. The painting is only 11.8 x 9.8 in.

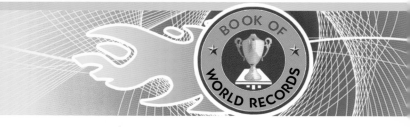

MOST EXPENSIVE PAINTING AT AUCTION

Pablo Picasso's *Nude, Green Leaves and Bust* (1932), set a record as the most expensive painting ever sold at auction when, on Monday May 3rd 2010, it sold for $106.5 million at Christie's International. The previous record was $104.2 million paid in 2004 for a 1905 Picasso painting, *Garcon a la Pipe*, at Sotheby's in New York. Sold to an undisclosed bidder, *Nude, Green Leaves and Bust* had been projected to sell for $70 million to $90 million. It has been reported that Picasso painted the painting in one day!

LARGEST ART AUCTION HOUSE

Christie's is currently the world's largest art auction house. Founded by James Christie in London on December 5, 1766, Christie's has auctioned works by the likes of Picasso, Rembrandt, da Vinci and Van Gogh. Sotheby's, founded by Samuel Barker in 1744, holds the record for being the oldest running art auction house. Sotheby's was also the first international art auction house to hold auctions on the Internet, from January 2000. Bonhams is the third largest art auction house.

LARGEST ART MUSEUM

With its vast collection of Oriental, Egyptian, Greek and Roman antiquities, as well as paintings, drawings and sculptures from all over the world, the Louvre in Paris holds the record for being the most visited and the largest art museum in the world. The Louvre houses the famous Mona Lisa. This iconic painting has a $7.5 million security system-protected room all of its own!

MOST SUCCESSFUL FEMALE RECORDING ARTIST

With an estimated worth of over $350 million, Madonna is the most successful and highest earning female recording artist of all time. She has many hit albums to her credit, including *Like a Virgin*, *True Blue*, *Like a Prayer* and *Ray of Light*.

MOST SUCCESSFUL ENTERTAINER

Michael Jackson holds the record for being the most successful entertainer of all time. Popularly known as the 'King of Pop', Jackson began his career in music at the age of seven. Michael Jackson's *Off the Wall* was the first album in history to produce four top-ten chart hits. With hit albums like *Thriller*, *Bad*, *Dangerous*, *History*, and *Blood on the Dance Floor* to his credit. Sadly, Michael Jackson died on June 25, 2009 at the age of 50.

Did you know?

Beethoven was a German composer and virtuoso pianist. He continued to compose his masterpieces and perform even after he lost his hearing.

MOST GRAMMY AWARDS

Sir George Solti, a famous British–Hungarian music conductor, has won the most number of Grammy awards. Solti has won a total of 31 Grammys and was nominated an additional 74 times before his death in 1997.

MOST CURTAIN CALLS

Italian tenor, Luciano Pavarotti, holds the record for the most curtain calls. The famous classical vocalist received 165 curtain calls — more than any other artist in the world. Pavarotti was one of the Three Tenors, who changed the face of operatic music. The other two tenors were Placido Domingo and Jose Carreras. Pavarotti also holds the record for the best selling classical album, *In Concert*.

BEST-SELLING MUSICAL GROUP

The famous British band *The Beatles* set several records during their recording career, many of which are yet to be broken. *The Beatles* are, to date, the best selling musical group. The band have sold over one billion albums worldwide. The group has also had more number one albums than any other band and have a record six diamond-selling albums to their credit.

SHORTEST PLAY IN THE WORLD

Lasting for about 25 seconds, The Breath, an Irish play by Samuel Beckett, holds the record for the shortest play in the world. It was first staged by Beckett in 1969, who is considered the father of the 'theatre of the absurd'.

Did you know?

The Phantom of the Opera is the longest running play to be performed on Broadway. It has been running for 22 years and counting since January 1988.

MOST PUBLISHED PLAYWRIGHT

William Shakespeare is the most published playwright in history. Interestingly, none of Shakespeare's plays were published in his lifetime. We read his plays today only because his fellow actors posthumously recorded his work as a dedication to their fellow actor in 1623, publishing 36 of Shakespeare's plays.

MOST SUCCESSFUL COMPOSER

Andrew Lloyd Webber is the most successful composer of musical theatre. Many of Webber's musicals have run for more than a decade. He is best-known for *Cats* and *The Phantom of the Opera.*

LONGEST PLAY IN THE WORLD

Running for a total of 22 hours, *The Warp*, by Neil Oram is the play with the longest duration. It is a series of 10 plays performed in sequence about an English mystic and his journey through life.

LONGEST RUNNING PLAY

The Mousetrap is the longest running theatrical play in the world. Originally called *The Three Blind Mice*, the play was written by Agatha Christie in 1947. A 30-minute radio play, it was written to celebrate the 80th birth anniversary of Queen Mary. The show opened in London in 1952 at the Ambassador's Theatre in London and has been running ever since. The play has been translated into 20 languages, performed in more than 40 countries over the world and watched by more than 10 million people. It was attended by the Queen Elizabeth II herself to celebrate her 50th year on the throne.

DIRECTOR WITH THE MOST OSCARS

John Ford is the only person to have received four Academy Awards for Best Director. He won the first award in 1935 for *The Informer*. Ford followed it up, winning two successive awards in 1940 and 1941, for *The Grapes of Wrath* and *How Green Was My Valley* respectively. The fourth award came in 1952 for *The Quiet Man*.

MOST OSCAR NOMINATIONS RECEIVED BY AN ACTOR

The actor to have received the most number of Oscar nominations is Meryl Streep. She has received 16 nominations and won on two occasions. Katherine Hepburn and Jack Nicholson follow closely with 12 nominations each and four and three awards respectively.

MOVIE WITH THE MOST OSCAR NOMINATIONS

The highest number of nominations received by a movie is a prize shared by two movies – *All About Eve* (1950) and *Titanic (1997)*. Both of these films received a stupendous 14 nominations each. Now considered a classic, *All About Eve* won six awards in 1950, including Best Picture. *Titanic* won an incredible 11 of its 14 nominations, including Best Picture and Best Director.

MOVIE WITH THE MOST OSCARS

The record for the highest number of Academy Awards won by a movie is shared by three movies – *Ben-Hur* (1959), *Titanic* (1997) and *The Lord of the Rings: Return of the King* (2003) – each winning 11 Oscars.

LONGEST RUNNING FILM SERIES

The longest running film series is James Bond. The first film, Dr. No, was released in 1962 and the series is still going strong, with Quantum of Solace being released in 2008. This series has seen six actors in the starring role and is one of the most financially successful movie franchises of all time.

ACTORS WITH MOST NUMBER OF OSCARS

Among the male actors there is a tie between Jack Nicholson and Walter Brennan. Both of whom have won three Oscars. Among female actors, Katherine Hepburn holds the record with four wins!

Did you know?

The world's largest film studio is the Ramoji Film City in Hyderabad, India. It spreads over 2.6 sq/miles (6.74 sq/km).

TELEVISION

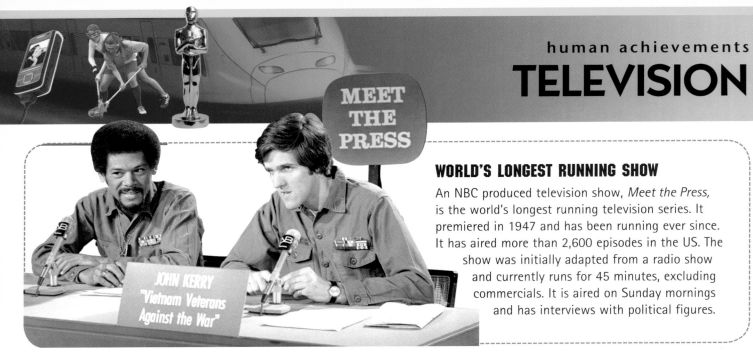

MEET THE PRESS

JOHN KERRY
"Vietnam Veterans
Against the War"

WORLD'S LONGEST RUNNING SHOW

An NBC produced television show, *Meet the Press*, is the world's longest running television series. It premiered in 1947 and has been running ever since. It has aired more than 2,600 episodes in the US. The show was initially adapted from a radio show and currently runs for 45 minutes, excluding commercials. It is aired on Sunday mornings and has interviews with political figures.

MOST EMMY AWARDS WON BY A TELEVISION SERIES

The highest number of Emmy Awards won by a television series is 109, awarded to *Sesame Street*. The American educational show for preschool children is considered a pioneer of contemporary educational television standards. No other series has matched its level of international recognition and success. It has been televised in over 120 countries and adapted into 30 international versions, excluding dubbed editions!

LONGEST RUNNING U.S. TV CARTOON

The Simpsons made their debut as a sitcom on December 17, 1989 and is now in their 20th season and going strong. However, they are far outdone by Japanese TV cartoon Sazae-san which premiered in Japan on October 5, 1969 and is still being shown every Sunday evening.

Did you know?

Frasier holds the record for the most primetime Emmy wins, winning 37! *Academy Awards* is a close second with 33 wins. *The Mary Tyler Moore Show* is third in the list, with 29 wins.

HIGHEST PAID PERSON ON TELEVISION

Oprah Winfrey is the highest paid star on television. According to recent reports, Oprah is estimated to have earned $350 million in 2009! She produces and hosts the award-winning television show, The Oprah Winfrey Show, which has remained the number one talk show for 22 consecutive seasons. Produced by Oprah's own production house, Harpo Productions, the show is seen by an estimated 46 million viewers every week in the US.

THE LONGEST RUNNING REALITY SHOW

MTV's The Real World first aired in 1992 and is believed by many to be the longest running reality show... but it's not- that honor goes to COPS. The show that follows police officers on the beat premiered on March 11, 1989.

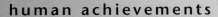

COUNTRIES AND PEOPLE

LARGEST CONTINENT BY POPULATION

Asia holds record for being the largest continent in terms of population. Home to almost 60 per cent of the population of the world, more than 4 billion people live here!

LARGEST COUNTRY BY POPULATION

With approximately 1.32 billion people, China has the highest population of any country in the world. The country's population is almost equal to 20 per cent of the world's population – so, almost 1 in 5 people in the world live in China! China's populace is very unevenly distributed, with almost 95 per cent of its people living in the southeast of the country.

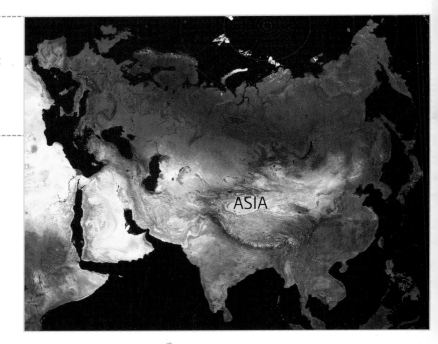

ASIA

Persons per square kilometer
0 1 10 100 200
Uninhibited
0 2.6 26 260 520
Persons per square mile

Beijing

CHINA   Shanghai

SMALLEST COUNTRY IN THE WORLD

The smallest country in the world is the Vatican. A country within a city, Vatican City's territory exists inside a walled enclave within the city of Rome, Italy. It has an area of about 110 acres and a population just over 800.

Did you know?

The most expensive shopping streets in the world are considered to be Fifth Avenue in New York, Causeway Bay in Hong Kong, the Champs Elysées in Paris and Oxford Street in London.

WORLD'S RICHEST MAN

Carlos Slim, a Mexican businessman and the richest man in the world. Estimatedly worth $53.5 billion, he beats Bill Gates by a mere half a billion dollars. Slim's family holdings control more than 5 per cent of Mexico's GDP. His wealth is built on a telecommunication service – spanning from the Dominican Republic to Chile – that boasts more than 100 million customers!

RICHEST CITY IN THE WORLD

The Japanese capital of Tokyo is believed to be the richest city in the world and, according to reports, will remain so till the year 2020. It is believed to have a GDP of $1.2 trillion, which will rise to $1.6 trillion by 2020. The second richest city in the world is New York.

MOST READ BOOK

The Bible has a recorded 3.9 billion copies in print. Written over 16 centuries it is an amazing collection of 66 books containing the word of God. The next most read book is Quotations from the Works of Mao Tse-Tung at 820 million followed by Harry Potter books at 400 million.

Did you know?

Borobudur, in Central Java, Indonesia, is the largest Buddhist temple in the world. For many centuries this beautiful tribute to Lord Buddha was buried under volcanic ash. It was later rediscovered by the British Governor-General of Java, Thomas Stamford Raffles, who was very interested in history. It is a place of pilgrimage for Mahayana Buddhists.

THE OLDEST PRACTICED RELIGION

The oldest practiced religion in the world today is Hinduism. It is commonly known as Sanatana Dharma and is the first among the Dharma faiths. Its origins can be traced back to the ancient Vedic culture and dates back as far as 2000 BC. Contemporary Hinduism is divided into four main divisions – Vaishnavism, Shaktism, Shaivism and Smartism.

RELIGION WITH THE MOST NUMBER OF FOLLOWERS

Christianity is the world's most practiced religion with more than 2 billion followers in the world. It has several branches, including Roman Catholic, Protestant, Anglican, Orthodox and several other independent streams.

BIGGEST TEMPLE

Angkor Wat, in Angkor, Cambodia, is the largest Hindu temple complex in the world. In fact, it is the largest religious monument ever built. It was built for King Suryavarman in the 12th century and served as the capital of the Khmer Empire from 802–1295. It is now a destination for tourists and Buddhist pilgrims.

WORLD'S YOUNGEST RELIGION

Baha'i is the world's youngest religion. It was founded by Baha'ullah in the 19th century. The religion has about six million followers in more than 200 countries across the world. The governing body of Baha'i is in Haifa, Israel.

Alternative: Choice

Auction house: A place where items are sold at bided prices

Celebrity: Famous person

Composer: A person who creates music.

Contemporary: Belonging to the present age

Converting: Changing

Cottage Industry: A small-scale industry

Dispatched: Sent off

Honor: To show respect

Incredible: Amazing

Installed: Connected or set in position

Invasion: Attack by enemies

Lighthouse: A tall tower near the coast that flashes light to guide ships and boats sailing by

Mesoamerica: A region and culture area in the Americas extending approximately from Mexico to Honduras and Nicaragua.

Mummified: To make into a mummy by embalming and drying to preserve dead bodies

Old master: A renowned European painter or painting completed before 1800

Patent: To get a grant by the government to have the sole right to make, use or sell one's own invention for a certain period of time

Phonetic: Representing sounds of speech

Pictograms: Picture symbols that stand for words

Pilgrimage: A journey to a holy place

Pith: Soft, spongy material inside the stems of plants

Precise: Accurate

Production car: Cars produced for general sale

Skyscraper: A very tall building

Spokes: Rods in a wheel

Successive: One after another

Suspension bridge: A bridge that is suspended from cables anchored to supporting towers

Tomb: A place of burial